CHRISTMAS IS COMING!

But Waiting Is Hard!

Family Activities and Devotions for Advent

CHRISTMAS IS COMING!
But Waiting Is Hard!

Family Activities and Devotions for Advent

KAREN WHITING

CHRISTMAS IS COMING!
BUT WAITING IS HARD!

ISBN: 9781501824722
PACP10041877-01

16 17 18 19 20 21 22 23 24 25 – 10 9 8 7 6 5 4 3 2 1

Printed in the United Sates of America

CONTENTS

God's Love Is an ADVENTure

And one of the best ADVENTures happens at Christmastime!

It's a time of joy!

It's a time of waiting!

It's a time of preparing our hearts for God's love!

Using an Advent wreath decorates our home and creates a focus to prepare our hearts for Christmas. It provides time daily to reflect on Jesus and what his coming means.

Consider the deeper meaning of the wreath, candles, evergreens, and other Christmas symbols; and discover the real joy of the season.

Intentional Choices to Prepare for Christmas

WALKING TOWARD the living room, I stopped in my tracks and listened to my children's voices:

"It's ruined now. Dad chopped off the best part!" Michael exclaimed.

"The top is still on, and it's still tall," James said.

"Look at it," Michael urged. "Dad chopped off the bottom, and the branches are too bushy. How can anything big fit under the tree now?"

Their words dispelled my dreams of the tree and decorations helping our children understand the meaning of Christmas. Our family had spent a cold, blustery Saturday seeking the perfect Christmas tree. We trudged onward in the biting winds until we found a tall, perfectly shaped, blue spruce. My husband, Jim, lifted his ax and whacked at the trunk. The tree toppled onto the snowy ground. We proudly carried the tree home and stood it in the center of our living room. Now I wondered, *What should we do with this evergreen spinner of materialistic dreams?*

I discovered God's word about an evergreen tree, in Hosea 14:8: "I am like an evergreen tree, yielding my fruit to you throughout the year. My mercies never fail" (TLB). Here the evergreen tree is a symbol of God, caring for and blessing God's children throughout the year.

I wanted to do more than point to the tree and say, "This is a picture of God." I wanted to be more mindful of the season and bring Jesus into all the days leading up to Christmas. The Advent wreath seemed like the perfect answer.

We started using the Advent wreath with a daily Scripture reading, a hymn, and discussion of the various Christmas symbols. In the glow of the candles, I saw our family settle down and focus on Jesus. I pray that these devotions and ideas will help your family create a more meaningful Christmas and fill your hearts with joy at Christ's birth.

WHAT IS AN ADVENT WREATH?

On that day, the Lord of heavenly forces will be a splendid garland and a beautiful wreath for the people who survive. Isaiah 28:5

Advent is the short form of the Latin words *adventus Domini,* meaning "the coming of the Lord." Jesus came! That's a great reason to celebrate.

The Advent wreath is made with evergreens and four candles that are equally spaced around the circle. A white candle, called the Christ Candle, is placed in the center.

Traditionally, the wreath is in the shape of a circle to represent our eternal God, who has no beginning and no end. The evergreens symbolize growth and eternal life.

Three of the four candles are usually purple as reminders of the royalty of Jesus our King. The third candle is pink to represent either Mary, the mother of Jesus, or Joy. A white candle is added to the center on Christmas Eve or Christmas Day to represent Jesus. This is called the Christ Candle.

One week at a time, a candle is lit for each Sunday before Christmas, until all four are lit on the final Sunday of Advent.

Each candle has a name and is associated with a virtue Jesus brings us: Hope, Love, Joy, and Peace. The Christ Candle reminds us that Jesus is the light of the world.

We believe that Jesus is the light who came into the world. The increasing light that glows each week on the Advent wreath reminds us how the light of Jesus overpowers the darkness of fear and sin.

Note: Candles should never be left burning without an adult in attendance. Be sure to put all candles out immediately after each family devotion.

Additional resources on Advent are available at karenwhiting.com.

MAKE AN ADVENT WREATH

SUPPLIES

- Real or artificial evergreens
- Wire
- Wire cutters
- Small candleholders (if not using an Advent wreath frame)
- Four candles for the wreath (usually three purple and one pink)
- Decorations, as desired (pinecones, ribbons, pompoms, artificial fruits, nuts)
- One white candle and candleholder for the center (add on Christmas Day)
- Optional: Advent wreath frame

DIRECTIONS

1. Twist the evergreens into a circle. Twist the wire around the evergreens, as needed, to hold the shape.

   Or, if using an Advent wreath frame, place the evergreens over the frame.
2. Add candleholders, evenly spaced around the circle, if you are not using an wreath frame that includes candleholders.
3. Place the four candles in the candleholders.
4. Decorate the wreath, using wire to attach the decorations.

USE IT

Each day, light the candle(s) for that week, read and discuss the devotion and Scriptures, pray together, sing a Christmas hymn, discuss the meaning of a Christmas symbol, and try the activity.

Hope
The Prophecy Candle

Therefore, the Lord will give you a sign. The young woman is pregnant and is about to give birth to a son, and she will name him Immanuel. Isaiah 7:14

CHRISTMAS IS COMING! BUT WAITING IS HARD!

Today is the beginning of Advent, and that's when our Christmas ADVENTure starts. Each day brings us a little closer to Christmas, when we celebrate Jesus' birth. Light the purple candle, opposite the pink one.

The angel Gabriel announced to Mary, "He will be great and he will be called the Son of the Most High." How exciting! But, after hearing this, Mary had to wait nine months to see Jesus and to hold him. Mary was not the first person to wait for Jesus to come. Prophets long ago told about his coming. The Israelites had waited centuries for the prophecies to be fulfilled, for the coming of Immanuel.

First, set up your Advent wreath. It's a circle of evergreens with four candles evenly spaced around the wreath. A circle has no beginning and no ending. That's like God's love!

The reason for Christmas is to celebrate Jesus. This first candle is called the Candle of Hope, or the Prophecy Candle. There's just a little glow, because we are just beginning the journey to Christmas.

There's no need to pack! It's a journey into your heart to discover more about God, who sent Jesus, the Son of God.

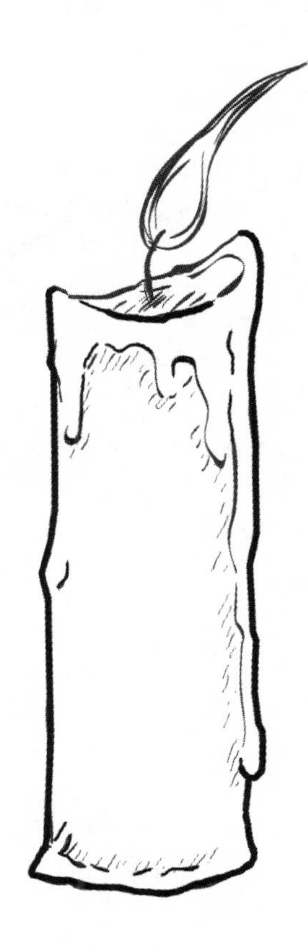

PRAYER

Thank you, God, for sending your Son, Jesus. Help us wait patiently for Christmas to come. Amen.

HYMN/SONG

"O Come, O Come, Emmanuel"

QUESTIONS

- What do you like about the Advent wreath?
- What does *Advent* mean?
- How will the wreath help us get ready for Christmas?

DID YOU KNOW?

Johann Hinrich Wichern created the first Advent wreath in 1839. He had founded a home for poor children, and they kept asking if it was Christmas yet. The Advent wreath helped the children keep track of the days remaining until Christmas.

TRY IT

Look up a prophecy and how it was fulfilled.

Prophecy: Isaiah 7:14
Fulfilled: Matthew 1:18–23

CHRISTMAS SYMBOL: WREATH

Dear friends, let's love each other, because love is from God, and everyone who loves is born from God and knows God. The person who doesn't love does not know God, because God is love. 1 John 4:7-8

Do you know that God loves you? God will always love you. A circle shape is a reminder of God's everlasting love. God also wants you to love other people.

Wreaths decorate doors with an inviting message of welcome. Wreaths were used in the ancient world, especially Greece. Wreaths of laurel were used as crowns to honor a person. In Germany, people used wreaths as a sign of hope for the coming of spring. In 1 Corinthians 9:25, Paul speaks of a crown that will never die.

TRY IT

Encircle each family member with your arms to give wreath-shaped hugs.

Micah's Prophecy

As for you, Bethlehem of Ephrathah, though you are the least significant of Judah's forces, one who is to be a ruler in Israel on my behalf will come out from you. His origin is from remote times, from ancient days. Micah 5:2

LONG AGO, Isaiah, Micah, and other prophets told people about the coming Messiah. Micah even told the people where the Messiah would be born. Wow! Every single prophesy happened as God had foretold it!

Christmas is good news because it shows God keeps promises and sent Jesus, the promised Messiah, to bring hope to the world. We share that hope when we tell others about Jesus and say, "Merry Christmas."

PRAYER

Dear Lord, help us share the hope of eternal life with others. Amen.

HYMN/SONG

"Mary Did You Know?"

QUESTIONS

- Why is it so great that God loves you?
- In what part of the world is Bethlehem? Can you find Israel and Bethlehem on a map?
- What prophets can you name?
- What is your hope for the future?

DID YOU KNOW?

The organization Wreaths Across America places wreaths on hundreds of thousands of veterans' graves in December to honor them.

TRY IT

Copy, cut out, and decorate the small Bible below and add it to the wreath as a reminder of the prophecies.

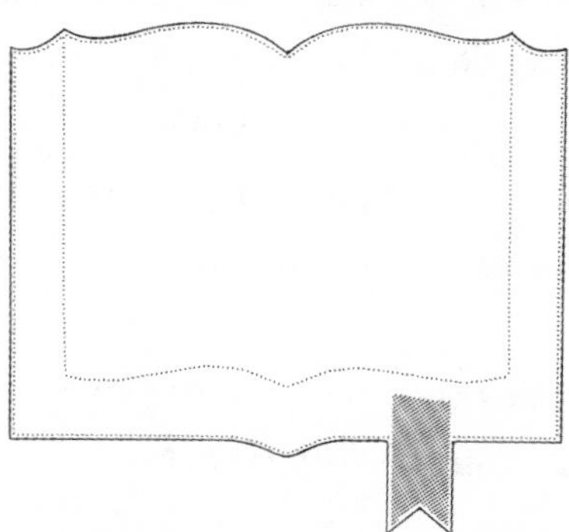

CHRISTMAS SYMBOL: CHRISTMAS TREE

I am like an evergreen tree, yielding my fruit to you throughout the year. My mercies never fail. (TLB)

Christmas trees transform a room into a holiday wonderland. God is compared to an evergreen tree in the Hosea passage. In some Bible translations, God is compared to a "luxuriant evergreen tree." God is splendid and extravagant.

The Christmas tree originated in Germany. There are a number of different stories about how the tree became a Christmas symbol. It may have started with the Paradise plays, where an evergreen tree hung with apples represented the garden of Eden. Or, it's said that Martin Luther brought an evergreen tree inside and decorated it with candles after noticing the beauty of one tree during a walk on Christmas Eve.

Hessian soldiers from Germany brought the tradition of the lighted evergreens to America during the American Revolution.

Let evergreen trees that point to the heavens remind you that you are part of God's family tree.

TRY IT

Make Christmas tree gift tags with notes of hope. You will need colored paper (variety of colors), ribbon, markers, scissors, paper punch, and Christmas tree cookie cutters (optional).

1. Copy the pattern below (or trace tree cookie cutters) on various colors of paper, and cut out the paper trees.
2. Stack three trees of different colors, punch a hole through the layers, and tie together with a ribbon.
3. Write "Merry Christmas" on the top card. Spread the other cards open and write on them "Jesus loves you" and other messages.

Prayer Wreath

Mary said, "With all my heart I glorify the Lord!" Luke 1:46

A WREATH is a circle of love. Mary visited Elizabeth, who also was expecting a baby. Mary responded to Elizabeth's greeting, but did not say, "Hooray for me!" Instead, Mary praised all the great things her mighty God did for her. Christmas is a time to praise God for the gift of Jesus and to be thankful for all that God has done.

Mary and Elizabeth must have hugged each other as they praised God together. When people come together to praise God, that creates a prayer circle or wreath.

Invite your family members to stand in a circle and to hold hands to form a family prayer wreath. Let one person pray aloud and, when done, gently squeeze the next person's hand. The person with the last hand squeezed says, "Amen."

In a prayer wreath, you may hold your dad's strong hand, a step-sister's ring-covered fingers, your mom's gentle hand, or a baby brother's chubby hand. As you hold on, remember that God has a firm grasp on your life.

PRAYER

Thank you, Jesus, for always making a prayer circle with us. Thanks for your everlasting love! Amen.

HYMN/SONG

"He's Got the Whole World in His Hands"

QUESTIONS

- Wreaths often are hung on doors as a sign of welcome. Read Revelation 3:20. Have you opened the door of your heart and let Jesus inside?
- What do you like about praying with your family?
- What are some things for which you can praise God?

DID YOU KNOW?

No one can separate you from God's love. Check it out in Romans 8:37-39.

TRY IT

Wrap your arms around yourself and say, "God loves me!"

CHRISTMAS SYMBOL: CHAINS AND GARLANDS

She will place a graceful wreath on your head; she will give you a glorious crown. Proverbs 4:9

Some people circle the tree with a festive garland. In Hawaii, people use flower garlands, called leis, to greet and honor guests. Early American settlers brought the custom of using garlands for Christmas decorations from England. They hung evergreen garlands on mantels and over doors.

Choose to make a special garland of loving deeds by adding a link for every act of love a family member does each day. The chain will lengthen as Christmas approaches. On Christmas Eve, wrap the chain around the tree to wrap the tree with love.

TRY IT

Make a chain of hearts.

1. Photocopy the pattern on page 23. Cut out the outer heart, fold on the line, and cut out the inner heart.
2. Fold paper in half, place the heart's fold on the paper's fold, trace the heart, and cut it out. Make many hearts, and cut through the bottom point on each heart.
3. Link two hearts, then staple or tape the bottom point closed on each one. Add more hearts to make a chain.

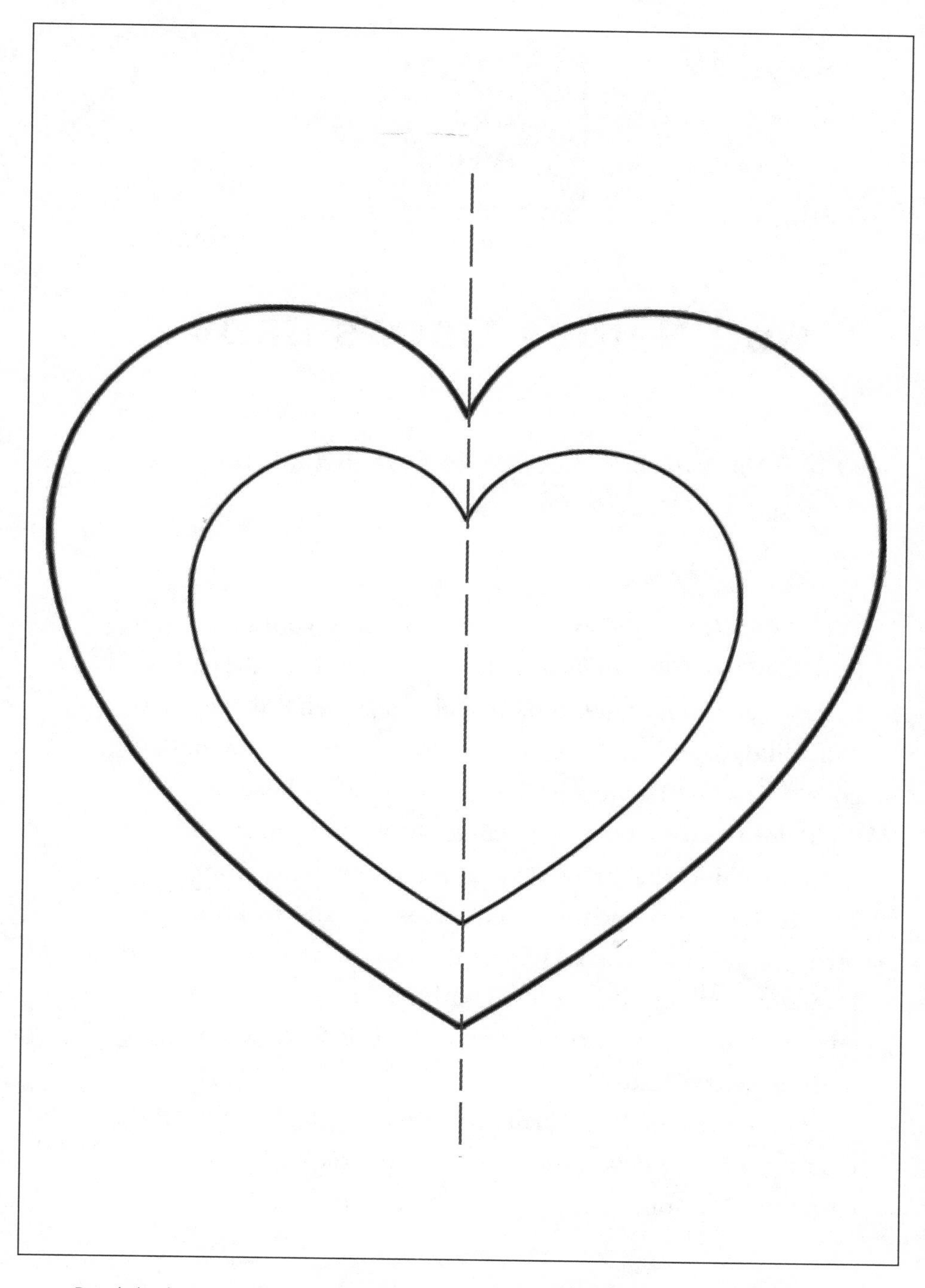

God Names Mary's Baby

Look! You will conceive and give birth to a son, and you will name him Jesus. Luke 1:31

YOUR FAMILY probably took time to choose your name. And they may have given you a nickname. Friends might call you by a special nickname, too. You also are called daughter or son, child, friend, and maybe sister or brother, grandchild, or cousin. Discuss how each person's name was chosen.

Before Mary's baby started to grow, the angel told her what to name the baby. The name came right from God! The name *Jesus* means "God saves." Jesus is known by other names, too. The Old Testament said he would be called Immanuel, which means "God with us." He also is known as Savior, Redeemer, Christ, and the Son of God. Each name helps describe Jesus.

The names of Jesus bring hope to the world and reflect God's power. Those are reasons to rejoice during the Christmas season.

PRAYER

Thank you, God, for the gift of Jesus. Thanks for helping my family choose my name. Amen.

HYMN/SONG

"Jesus, Name Above All Names" or "The Only Name"

QUESTIONS

- The Ten Commandments include a rule about not using God's name the wrong way (Exodus 20:7). This also means being careful using the name of Jesus. How should you use God's name?
- What's your favorite name for Jesus and why?

DID YOU KNOW?

Jesus told us to pray in his name (John 15:16).

TRY IT

Copy and cut out the scroll. Decorate the scroll with your name to make an ornament. Add the ornament to the tree as a reminder that you're part of God's family tree.

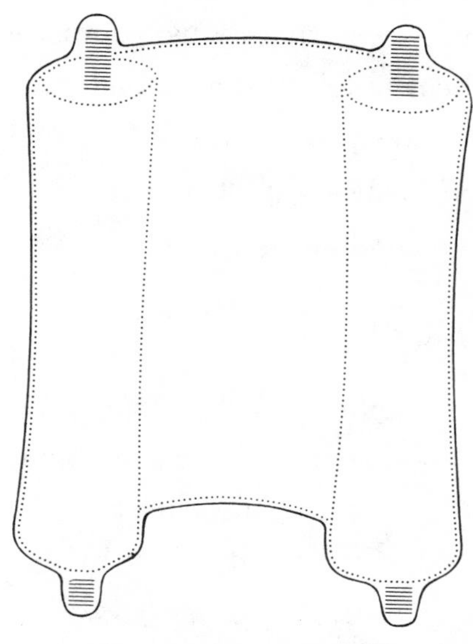

CHRISTMAS SYMBOL: THE JESSE TREE

A shoot will grow up from the stump of Jesse; a branch will sprout from his roots. Isaiah 11:1

Jesse is the name of one of Jesus' ancestors. *Jesse* means "Yahweh exists." The Jesse Tree shows the important ancestors of Jesus, starting with Adam. The tradition started in the Middle Ages and came from today's Scripture, a prophesy that Jesus would come from the root of Jesse and bear much fruit and that the Lord's spirit would be on him.

It's a story in symbols that tells us about the family tree of Jesus. Symbols include an apple for Adam and Eve, an ark for Noah, a tree root for Jesse, and a harp for King David.

TRY IT

Make Jesse Tree ornaments.

- Copy the patterns on page 27, cut them out, and decorate a harp (the symbol for David) and an ark (the symbol for Noah).
- Look up the Jesse Tree online. Make other Jesse Tree ornaments, and discuss the meaning of each.

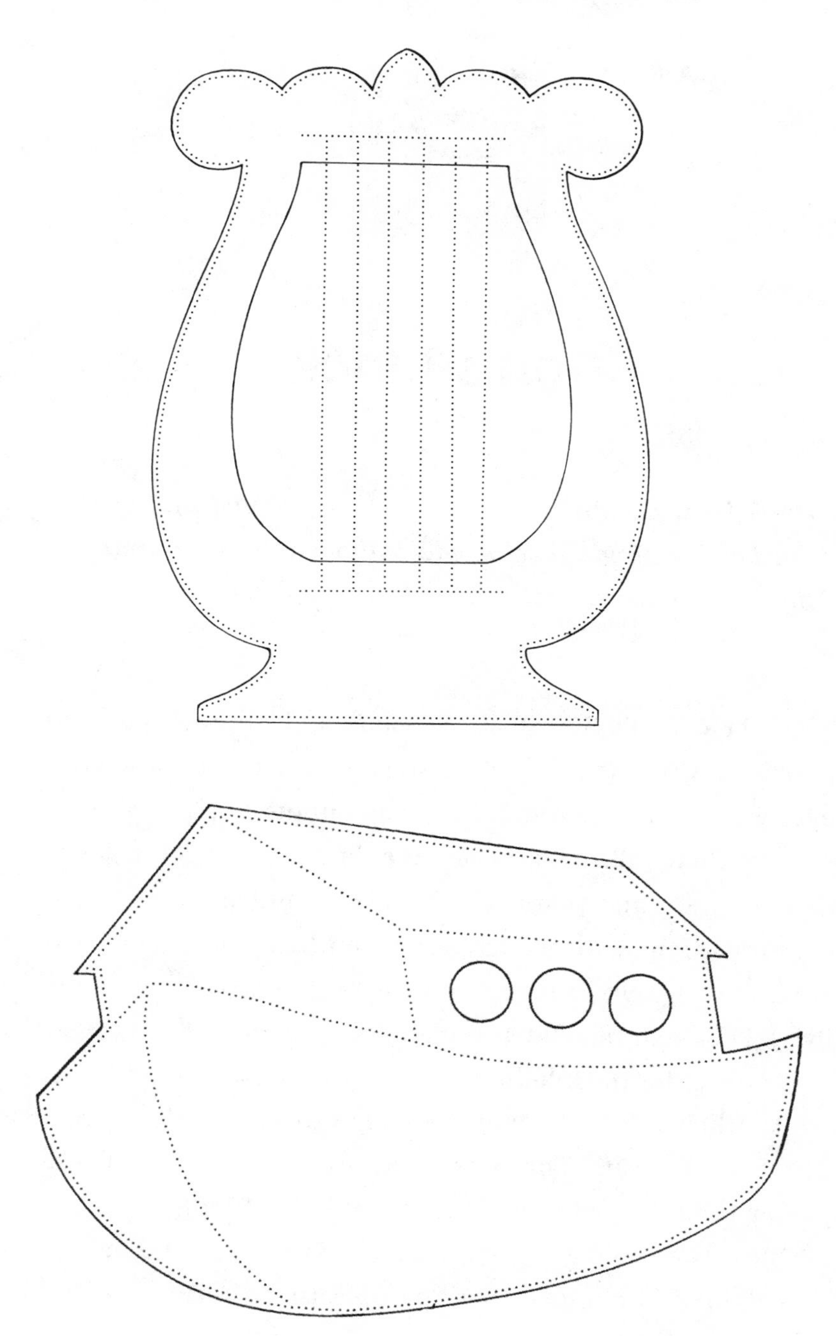

God's Clock

Don't let it escape your notice, dear friends, that with the Lord a single day is like a thousand years and a thousand years are like a single day. 2 Peter 3:8

TICK-TOCK! TICK-TOCK! Seconds and minutes seem to pass so slowly when you're waiting for Christmas. Close your eyes while someone watches for one minute to pass.

The Bible talks about time in a different way. One day is like one thousand years. That's called a millennium. It's ten centuries. Ten centuries ago would be when your great-great-great-great-great—well, make that a lot of greats—grandparents lived. People in the Old Testament waited through a number of centuries for the fulfillment of God's promise to send Jesus.

Matthew 1 lists the main people in the generations, from Abraham to Jesus. That was a gigantic time to wait. These people remained faithful believers as they waited.

Just twenty-five days before Christmas is 600 hours. That's 36,000 minutes. How many of those will you spend thinking about Jesus?

PRAYER

Lord, thank you for keeping your promises. Help us be faithful in believing in you. Amen.

HYMN/SONG

"O Come, All Ye Faithful"

QUESTIONS

- When has it been hard to wait?
- When does the time seem to go fast?
- What people do you know in different generations in your family?
- What can you do in one minute?

DID YOU KNOW?

There are forty-two generations from Abraham to Jesus.

TRY IT

Make a promise to God of spending time each day praying or reading the Bible.

CHRISTMAS SYMBOL: ANGEL TREE

You know the grace of our Lord Jesus Christ. Although he was rich, he became poor for our sakes, so that you could become rich through his poverty. 2 Corinthians 8:9

Many churches decorate trees with angels and notes. These are called Angel Trees. Different organizations send in names for Angel Trees, including prisons and groups that work with people in need.

Angel Trees also remind us that Jesus lived in a poor family. Jesus, the Son of God, became poor to help us look beyond money to what's more important: life and God's gift of eternal life.

Giving to a child in need is a way to honor Jesus and to show generosity to God.

TRY IT

Find an Angel Tree, choose a few names, and shop for those children. Add a little extra, such as a bow or baseball cap to match a T-shirt or a toy to put with clothes. Consider that you are shopping for Jesus and his friends when you shop for a child.

H-O-P-E

When the fulfillment of the time came, God sent his Son, born through a woman, and born under the Law. Galatians 4:4

ONE HOLY NIGHT long ago, a child's cry broke the silence as he took his first breath. No one but his parents heard the cry of this child, the newborn King.

Be still and let a few minutes of silence fill your heart. Then think about Jesus. Be humbled as you realize Jesus wants to fill your heart with love and hope.

Jesus also calls us to be the light of the world, to bring the hope of Jesus to others. Think of hope as an acrostic for *H*elping *O*ther *P*eople *E*ternally.

Lasting hope means believing that you will live with God forever. Share the good news that starts with the birth of Jesus and is fulfilled with his death and resurrection.

The lone candle on the Advent wreath is a beacon of light, inviting us to look toward God. Soon, more light will be added as our hope grows and Christmas draws closer.

PRAYER

Jesus, help us share real hope with others this Christmas season. Amen.

HYMN/SONG

"Breath of Heaven" or "Silent Night"

QUESTIONS

- Who do you know who needs real hope?
- How do you feel when the Advent candle is lit?
- What does hope mean to you?

DID YOU KNOW?

Before Jesus, many people in Scandinavia lit candles on a wheel to pray for the sun's return. In their far north countries, the sun rises only for a few hours each day in the winter. They wanted the sun to stay in the sky longer. There are still many people who don't know Jesus and put their hope in things. Share the true God and true light that brings real hope.

TRY IT

Wear a silly pin that lights up, and use it as a conversation starter to chat about Jesus being the true light.

CHRISTMAS SYMBOL: CHRISTMAS CARDS

Everyone who heard it was amazed at what the shepherds told them. Luke 2:18

Angels first shared the news of the Savior's birth when they appeared to shepherds in Bethlehem. The shepherds rushed from watching their sheep to find Jesus. Then they returned to their fields and praised God. And all the people who heard wondered about what the shepherds told them. Since that time, people have shared news about Jesus; however, Christmas cards are a fairly new custom.

Sir Henry Cole created the first official Christmas cards, in 1843, in London. He had one thousand cards made. The card showed a family celebration plus two panels of people sharing food and clothes with people in need. He designed cards to make people aware of the needs of the poor.

Christmas cards and spoken "Merry Christmas" greetings are still great opportunities to share about Jesus.

TRY IT

Make a cutout heart Christmas card.

1. Fold two sheets of paper in half. In the center of one, cut a heart without cutting through the heart's point.
2. Cut a heart inside the first one, leaving the points of both hearts attached. Do this a couple more times.
3. Open the heart paper.
4. Decorate the other paper (outside of the card).
5. Glue the back of the heart page inside the card, leaving the hearts unglued. Open the card so that the hearts pop up.

Another Child Is Coming!

He will make ready a people prepared for the Lord.
Luke 1:17

THE BOOK OF LUKE opens with an announcement of a baby, but it's not Jesus. The angel Gabriel told Zechariah, a priest, that he and his wife, Elizabeth, would have a son named John. That's John the Baptist, born six months before Jesus. God sent two babies.

When John grew up, he told people that Jesus the Messiah would come soon. John called out, "Prepare the way for the Lord." He told them to change their hearts and lives. He baptized them. He even baptized Jesus, announcing that Jesus was the one God sent.

Moms and Dads prepare for a new baby. They buy baby items, make a place for the baby to sleep, and choose a name. Christmas is the time when Christians prepare to celebrate Jesus' birthday. Some plan a birthday party for Jesus, and many decorate with a Nativity set as a reminder of Jesus and the people who came to see him. God sent Jesus to restore hearts, and the best preparation still is to prepare your heart.

PRAYER

Lord Jesus, help us change our hearts and lives. Help us prepare for your birthday. Amen.

HYMN/SONG

"Away in a Manger"

QUESTIONS

- Who did God send to prepare for the coming of Jesus, and what did that person do?
- What can you tell about each figure in the Nativity set?
- How are you preparing your heart for Christmas?

DID YOU KNOW?

After visiting the birthplace of Jesus, St. Francis of Assisi set up a live scene of the Nativity in a cave, in 1223. He used the Nativity to remind people of the reason to celebrate Christmas.

TRY IT

Ask God to forgive you and to restore your heart.

Copy and cut out the heart below. Decorate the heart and add it to your tree.

CHRISTMAS SYMBOL: NATIVITY SET

She gave birth to her firstborn child, a son, wrapped him snugly, and laid him in a manger, because there was no place for them in the guestroom. Luke 2:7

We celebrate Christmas to remember that God sent the promised Messiah. Nativity sets depict Jesus' birth. The word *nativity* is Latin and means "to be born." Churches started using Nativity sets during the early 1300s. At first, real people and animals put on a scene. Later, people used carved figures.

Nativity sets often include a stable or cave. Baby Jesus is placed in a manger, and the other figures are placed around the manger. A manger is a feeding trough or box for animals. Some people wait and add Jesus on Christmas Day.

TRY IT

You may have a few Nativity sets, including unbreakable ones for children. Try some of these activities to make the most of your Nativity set:

- Add one piece to the set daily to focus on that animal or person. Make the sounds of the animals and discuss how those animals help people.
- Move figures toward the set throughout Advent. This helps children understand that Mary and Joseph traveled to Bethlehem and how and when other people came.
- Place Jesus in a little box and giftwrap him in tissue paper to illustrate that God sent Jesus to us as a special promised gift. When you place Jesus in the manger, read John 3:16.

Love
The Bethlehem Candle

As for you, Bethlehem of Ephrathah, though you are the least significant of Judah's forces, one who is to be a ruler in Israel on my behalf will come out from you. His origin is from remote times, from ancient days. Micah 5:2

WE LIGHT a second candle this week. Two candles make a brighter glow as Christmas comes closer. The second candle is called the Candle of Love, or the Bethlehem Candle. The widow Ruth came to Bethlehem because of her love for her mother-in-law, Naomi. Jesus' birth took place in Bethlehem.

Bethlehem means "house of bread." It's a place where grain for bread grew. Bread is important in the Bible. The Israelites placed bread in the temple as a sign of God's presence. Jesus called himself the bread of life. In the early church, people met and broke bread together daily (Acts 2:42). The word *companion* means "one who breaks bread with another."

God carefully chose the place for Jesus' birth, even to a name that fit so well.

PRAYER

Thank you, Jesus, for being the bread of life. Be our daily bread. Amen.

HYMN/SONG

"O Little Town of Bethlehem"

QUESTIONS

- Read Ruth 1:16. How did Ruth show love to Naomi? What are some ways we can show love to others?
- *Companion* is a word we use for *friend.* How is another believer a special friend or a real companion?
- What makes Bethlehem so special for the birthplace of Jesus?

DID YOU KNOW?

In 2012, archaeologists uncovered an Israeli seal that states, "From the town of Bethlehem to the King." This was the first time the name Bethlehem appeared outside the Bible.

TRY IT

Make square and triangle slices of toast. Place a triangle slice on top of a square one to make a house of bread.

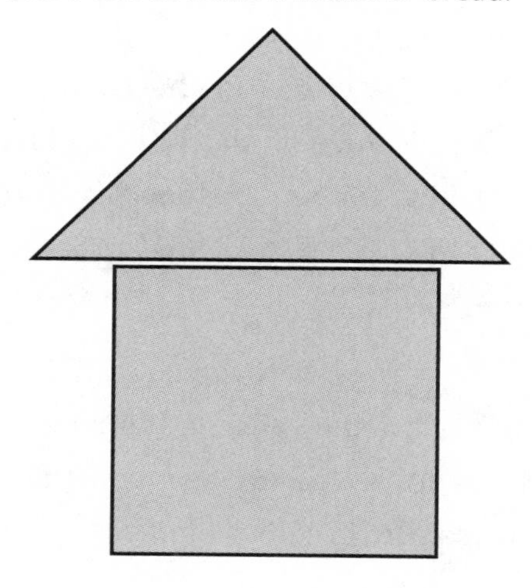

CHRISTMAS SYMBOL: CHRISTMAS BREADS

Jesus replied, "I am the bread of life. Whoever comes to me will never go hungry, and whoever believes in me will never be thirsty." John 6:35

German Christstollen, Slovak Sweet Bobalki, Norwegian Julekake, Italian Panettone, Spanish Rosca de Reyes (King's Cake), Scandinavian Wreath Bread, and French Bûche de Noël are Christmas breads or cakes served in various countries. Christstollen is shaped to resemble the swaddled baby Jesus. *Panettone* comes from words that mean "luxury cake." Other breads are braided and shaped like crowns or decorated with bright candied fruit to represent jewels. It's fitting to celebrate the season with bread.

Bread was a main part of the diet of the Israelites and during the days Jesus walked on the earth. People ate it daily and also made special breads for celebrations. King David gave bread cakes to his people to celebrate when he won back God's chest (ark of the covenant). The chest contained manna, the bread from heaven that God sent the people for forty years as they wandered in the desert.

When you pray the words in the Lord's Prayer "give us the bread we need for today" (Matthew 6:11), think of how it is also a prayer asking for the presence of Jesus, the bread of life, in your daily life.

TRY IT

Try making (or buying) and eating some type of special Christmas bread. Have an agape meal (love feast) to celebrate Jesus, the bread of life.

MINI ROSCA DE REYES (KING'S CAKE)

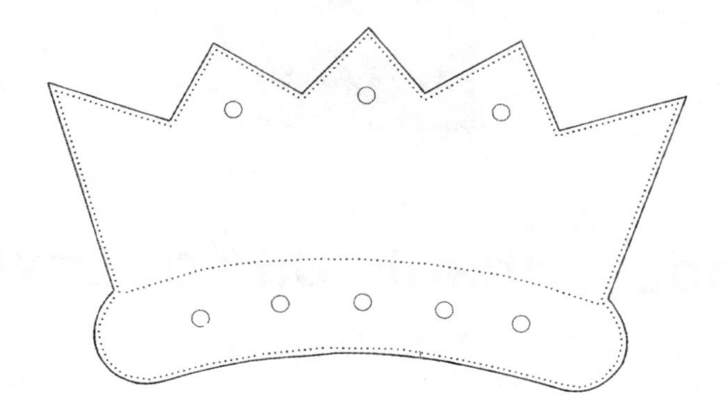

INGREDIENTS

Canned cinnamon rolls with icing
Purple, gold, and green colored sugar or sprinkles

DIRECTIONS

Preheat oven to 350 degrees.
Lightly grease a baking sheet.

1. Open the canned cinnamon rolls.
2. Separate the dough into rolls.
3. Unroll each roll to make a snake-like shape.
4. Fold each dough snake in half.
5. Twist each dough into a spiral.
6. Use the spiral to form a circle on the baking sheet.
7. Bake 20-25 minutes.
8. Spread the icing on the warm cakes.
9. Sprinkle the colored sugars or sprinkles on top of the icing.

Indescribable Gift of Love

Thank God for his gift that words can't describe!
2 Corinthians 9:15

WHAT'S THE BEST gift you have ever received? What gift do you hope to get this Christmas? What happened to last year's Christmas gifts? Did you break them or outgrow them? Do you still use a few? In the end, they are only objects and will not last forever. God sent a gift that lasts forever.

Jesus Christ is the gift of indescribable love and grace. Scriptures tell us that no one can tell how wonderful it really is. God is more than we can imagine. God's love is greater than we can understand. No words describe the depth of God's love. We know God loved us enough to send Jesus. We know God loves us enough to listen to us always. We know God loves us forever. God loves us enough to forgive us.

God loves us so much that God sent the Holy Spirit to be with us. Long before your birth, God loved you so much that God sent Jesus.

PRAYER

Lord, help us have a blessed Christmas and remember your gift of love today. Amen.

HYMN/SONG

"O Holy Night" or "When Love Came Down"

QUESTIONS

- Why is Jesus such a special gift?
- How much does God love you?
- How much does Jesus love you?

DID YOU KNOW?

No person has impacted history as much as Jesus.

TRY IT

Decorate a night light.

- Copy, cut out, and decorate the gift box on page 45.
- Tape the gift box to the outside of a night light as a reminder that Jesus is the best gift.
- Let the light that shines through the night be a reminder that Jesus is always with you.

CHRISTMAS SYMBOL: CANDLES

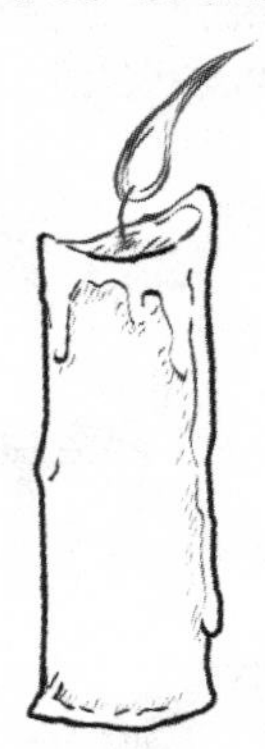

You are the light of the world. A city on top of a hill can't be hidden. Matthew 5:14

God gave us a wonderful gift at Christmas. But God doesn't want us to be selfish and keep it to ourselves. God calls us to be lights. As the shepherds told others about Jesus, so God wants us to tell others. We are to be lights. We light candles during Advent as reminders of Jesus, our light.

Be a light. Believe in Jesus and follow his teachings in the Bible.

Be like the light. Jesus was loving, forgiving, and a servant. Be like him. Love others with your words and actions. Forgive those who hurt you. Serve others with kind acts.

Jesus prayed. Remember to pray. Pray for others to know Jesus.

Share your faith.

TRY IT

Put a battery or solar light in a window (perhaps in each bedroom window) as a reminder to be a light.

Room for Jesus

Jesus replied, "Foxes have dens, and the birds in the sky have nests, but the Human One has no place to lay his head." Matthew 8:20

KNOCK! KNOCK! No, it wasn't a joke. Joseph tried to find a room for Mary to give birth to Jesus. But the town of Bethlehem was filled up, with not one room left for them. Joseph didn't give up looking for a safe place. He found shelter with the animals and used a manger for Jesus' bed. The manger, which often was made from stone, was the container for the animal's food. They camped out, and life began for Jesus in a humble place.

When Jesus grew up and began his ministry, he again had no place to call home. He moved around to help people and to talk to them. People mattered more to him than things and houses. Jesus wants to have a home in people's hearts.

Make sure you have room for Jesus at Christmas. Spend time each day praying and thinking about Jesus. Make sure there's room in your heart for Jesus all year. Tell Jesus that you believe in him and want him to be with you always.

PRAYER

Jesus, thanks for coming. I believe in you and want you to be in my heart and with me every day. Amen.

HYMN/SONG

"Thou Didst Leave Thy Throne"

QUESTIONS

- What do you believe about Jesus?
- How do you feel about your home?
- What animals have you watched eating? Where is their food placed?

DID YOU KNOW?

At the time of Jesus' birth, people made mangers from clay mixed with straw or from stones and mud. Sometimes people carved mangers from large rocks.

TRY IT

Decorate your bedroom door with a sign that says you have room for Jesus. Or copy, cut out, and decorate the doorknob hanger on page 49. You will need to cut a slit in the top, put it on the doorknob, and tape it closed.

CHRISTMAS SYMBOL: CHRISTMAS VILLAGE

God so loved the world that he gave his only Son, so that everyone who believes in him won't perish but will have eternal life. John 3:16

Many people display Christmas villages or scenes. Some even have train sets surrounding the village. Choo! Choo!

The tradition of setting up villages dates back to the Renaissance, when people started adding figures of all the people in a town to expand Nativity sets. The University of Dayton displays over two hundred Nativities that include figures from Ghana, Australia, Rwanda, and Poland.

In America, Christmas village displays began when Pennsylvania's Moravian believers set up "putz" displays. The word *putz* means "to decorate." People placed boxes shaped like houses around the Nativity set. Over the years, these scenes grew and people added many other figures, including skaters, cars, lampposts, and other items found in a city or town.

A village reminds us that God sent Jesus to all people from every city, town, and village in the world. It's fun to add new houses, especially houses from other countries.

TRY IT

Decorate small boxes as houses for a village.

- Use clay to make a tiny manger to add to the scene.
- Look up information about children around the world and the homes they live in.

Welcome,
Jesus!

King of Kings

After Jesus was born in Bethlehem in the territory of Judea during the rule of King Herod, magi came from the east to Jerusalem. They asked, "Where is the newborn king of the Jews? We've seen his star in the east, and we've come to honor him." Mathew 2:1-2

THE MAGI (wise men) were astronomers from the east. They studied a special star in the sky that led them to Jesus, the newborn King. God is so wise that the star was placed where even astronomers from another part of the world could see it!

The magi stopped during the journey at the palace of King Herod in Jerusalem and asked about the newborn King. Herod had the scribes of Israel investigate. These scribes pointed to the prophecy of Micah of the King's birth in Bethlehem.

The magi continued on to Bethlehem and found Jesus. They honored Jesus with gifts of gold, frankincense, and myrrh. The magi remind us again that God sent Jesus to all people. God's love is for everyone.

PRAYER

God, thank you for Jesus. Help us honor Jesus by sharing your love with others. Amen.

HYMN/SONG

"Do You Hear What I Hear?" or "Glory to the Newborn King"

QUESTIONS

- What do you think a king or great leader does for people? What does Jesus do?
- How is Jesus your king?
- What gifts can you bring to Jesus?

DID YOU KNOW?

The magi brought Jesus gifts considered appropriate for a king. Gold was considered valuable at the time of Jesus' birth for the same reason it's considered valuable today. Frankincense and myrrh were used as incense. Frankincense also was used in medications. Myrrh was used in preparing bodies for burial.

TRY IT

Copy, cut out, and decorate a crown ornament for your tree.

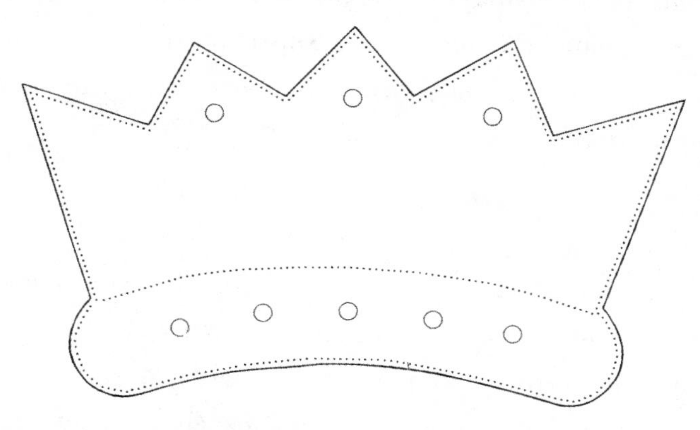

CHRISTMAS SYMBOL: CROWN

They dressed him up in a purple robe and twisted together a crown of thorns and put it on him. Mark 15:17

At Christmas, crowns remind us of Jesus our King and the magi who visited Jesus after his birth. A crown is a symbol of victory. In the original Olympics of the ancient world, the winners received crowns woven of leaves.

The magi recognized Jesus as a king, even in the humble setting of a house. At the time of the Crucifixion, soldiers wrote "king of the Jews" on the cross above Jesus' head. They placed a crown of thorns on his head as a way to tease and bully him. Over time, the thorns have become a way to recall that Jesus gave everything for us.

People started using holly at Christmas to replace a pagan tradition of using mistletoe. The sharp points of the holly remind people of the sharp pricks of thorns, and the berries are reminders that Jesus died for us.

TRY IT

Copy, cut apart, decorate, and tape together the strips on page 53 to make a crown. Add plain paper strips if needed. Or make a crown from paper, garlands, or evergreens. Then have a parade to celebrate Jesus, the newborn King.

Seed and Root of David

The man named his wife Eve because she is the mother of everyone who lives. Genesis 3:20

LET'S LOOK at the beginning of the Bible. In Genesis 2, God forms the first man and woman and places them in the garden of Eden. But the man and woman disobey God and, as a result, have to leave the garden. The man was named Adam. Adam named his wife Eve because she was to be the mother of everyone who lives.

While Matthew 1 begins the lineage of Jesus with Abraham, Luke 3:23-38 lists the parents and children, beginning with Jesus and going back to Adam. The verses in Luke end with "son of Enos son of Seth son of Adam son of God." The lineage of Jesus ultimately goes back to God.

Both Matthew and Luke include David in the lineage of Jesus. Jesus called himself the Son of David. When Jesus entered Jerusalem riding on a donkey, the crowds shouted, "Hosanna to the Son of David! Blessings on the one who comes in the name of the Lord!" (Matthew 21:9).

PRAYER

Thank you, God, for your Son, Jesus. We rejoice that because of Jesus we can call ourselves children of God. Amen.

HYMN/SONG

"God Rest Ye Merry Gentlemen"

QUESTIONS

- How is a baby like a seed or root?
- Talk about people in the family tree of Jesus.
- Talk about promises made and kept.

DID YOU KNOW?

Archaeological evidence of King David include a stone fragment with an inscription, called Tel Dan inscription, with the words "House of David" as well as the remains of a palace in Jerusalem that dates to the time of David.

TRY IT

Record each family member telling about what being a child of God means to him or her.

CHRISTMAS SYMBOL: FRUITS, SEEDS, AND CENTERPIECES

I, Jesus, have sent my angel to bear witness to all of you about these things for the churches. I'm the root and descendant of David, the bright morning star. Revelation 22:16

At Christmas, decorations may include bowls filled with holly, pinecones, and bright colored fruits. Pinecones are the seeds of evergreen trees. Birds and other creatures eat seeds, and many people coat pinecones with peanut butter and roll them in seeds to hang on trees for feathered creatures. Seeds and fruit can become reminders of new life, even in the midst of winter.

Seeds also remind us that Jesus would die and be changed. In John 12:23-24, Jesus compares his death to a grain of wheat dying in the ground and then sprouting with new life, growing, and producing many seeds. Jesus, the Son of God, knew he would die. He also knew he would rise to bring new life. Every seed holds the promise of life to come. It must be planted for the life to grow. Jesus came to give us all life that would last forever.

TRY IT

Fill a bowl with fruits and seeds, and make pinecone seed treats for birds.

Lighting the Way

A man named John was sent from God. He came as a witness to testify concerning the light, so that through him everyone would believe in the light. John 1:6-7

GOD SENT an angel to tell Zechariah that he would have a son named John, who would prepare people for Jesus. John, the son of Elizabeth, leaped inside his mother when Mary visited with Jesus growing inside her.

John the Baptist called people to change their hearts and to prepare for the Messiah. John referred to Jesus as the Lamb of God. When Jesus was an adult, John baptized him. After the baptism, the heavens opened and God said, "This is my Son whom I dearly love" (Matthew 3:17).

At Christmas we are happy Jesus came, because we know he came to save us and to be our guiding light. Turn off the electric lights and let the Advent wreath's candlelight fill the room. Remember that Jesus wants to fill your heart with his light. Jesus wants us to be lights that share our faith in Jesus. Jesus wants us to be like John and turn the hearts of people back to God.

PRAYER

Jesus, be our light. Help us share the message of Christ our Savior. Amen.

HYMN/SONG

"This Little Light of Mine"

QUESTIONS

- How can you share about Jesus today?
- Talk about John the Baptist and baptism.
- What does it mean to change your heart?

DID YOU KNOW?

The Lamb of God referred to the pure lamb used as the Passover sacrifice.

TRY IT

Play flashlight tag and talk about the importance of light, including the light of Jesus.

CHRISTMAS SYMBOL: LIGHTS

Jesus spoke to the people again, saying, "I am the light of the world. Whoever follows me won't walk in darkness but will have the light of life." John 8:12

Christmas lights add a brightness and color to the darker days of winter. Adding lights to Christmas trees started in the seventeenth century. Germans dripped wax on tree branches to stick the candles onto the tree. Candles can easily cause a tree to catch on fire, so people switched to electric lights when they became available.

Jesus called himself the light of the world. He adds brightness to our hearts in a world filled with trouble. Sadly, just as people take down Christmas lights and pack them away, they tend to put Jesus out of their minds and the Bible out of sight during much of the year. Be sure to stay connected to the real power, Jesus, all year.

TRY IT

Decorate the Christ Candle that will be used on Christmas Day. Use ribbons, silk flowers, or other tiny objects. Straight pens can be used to attach the items to the candle. Write your names on the ribbon as reminders that Christ came for each of you.

Ruth and Boaz of Bethlehem

Thus Naomi returned. And Ruth the Moabite, her daughter-in-law, returned with her from the territory of Moab. They arrived in Bethlehem at the beginning of the barley harvest. Ruth 1:22

THE BOOK OF RUTH tells about a woman named Ruth. She was a Moabite, descended from Lot, the nephew of Abraham. Her people became enemies of the Israelites.

Ruth married an Israelite, but he died, leaving her poor. Ruth moved to Bethlehem with her mother-in-law, Naomi. Ruth went to the fields to pick up leftover grain for food.

Ruth's story ended happily. Boaz, the owner of the field, saw Ruth and noticed her kindness. Boaz married Ruth. They had a son they named Obed, who married and had a son named Jesse. Jesse married and had many sons, including David, who became king of Israel. Since Jesus is descended from David, that means that he also is descended from Ruth and Boaz. The love story that took place in Bethlehem in a field led to Jesus. God used many people to fulfill the promise.

PRAYER

Almighty God, we are thankful that you use ordinary people for great purposes. Bless us and use us where you need us. Amen.

HYMN/SONG

"Christ Is Born in Bethlehem"

QUESTIONS

- Do you recall what the word *Bethlehem* means? What did people grow there, and what is it used to make?
- How did Ruth get food to eat? Was she rich or poor?
- What do you do to help poor people have food?

DID YOU KNOW?

Ruth did what was called gleaning. God told the people to leave what falls as they harvest food (gleanings) for the poor (Leviticus 19:9-10). In many communities, something similar takes place. Restaurants and grocery stores offer unsold day-old bread and other foods to food pantries and shelters.

TRY IT

Give non-perishable food to a food pantry or shelter.

CHRISTMAS SYMBOL: CHRISTMAS PAGEANTS AND CANTATAS

A record of the ancestors of Jesus Christ, son of David, son of Abraham. Matthew 1:1

In many churches, people hold performances at Christmas that share songs, stories, and plays related to the birth of Jesus. Some might even use Ruth's story as part of the show.

Mystery plays began in the Middle Ages (or Medieval times) and focused on Bible stories, including the birth of Jesus. They helped people who could not read understand important stories of the Bible. Tradesmen in guilds chose and performed stories related to their work. So, carpenter's guilds performed the building of Noah's ark, and goldsmiths performed the visit of the magi. Farmers might have performed the story of Ruth and Boaz.

Singing Scriptures or acting out part of a Bible story helps people remember the story.

TRY IT

Choose part of the Christmas story and create your own show. Make some props or scenery. Add songs. Record the show.

Joy
The Shepherd Candle

Nearby shepherds were living in the fields, guarding their sheep at night. Luke 2:8

THIS IS THE THIRD week of Advent. Light three candles this week, including the pink one. The lights on the wreath glow brighter. The pink candle is called the Candle of Joy. Knowing Christmas is so much closer brings more joy. It's also called the Shepherd Candle to remember the first people who visited Jesus.

That first Christmas, like most nights, the shepherds watched their sheep under the stars. They probably knew the stars and constellations well. Then they saw something strange appear in the sky. Not a UFO, but heavenly beings. At first, one angel appeared and spoke to the shepherds. Then a multitude of angels filled the sky to praise God. Heavenly sounds of worship gave glory to God.

People considered shepherds lowly people, of little value, but God chose them to be the first people to hear about the birth of Jesus. It became a night to remember and to share.

PRAYER

Lord, help us give glory to you and praise you each night. Amen.

HYMN/SONG

"While Shepherds Watched Their Flocks by Night"

QUESTIONS

- What do shepherds do?
- What constellations can you recognize?
- How would you feel if you saw an angel? Why do you think the first words angels spoke usually were "Don't be afraid"?

DID YOU KNOW?

Sheep are the most frequently mentioned animal in the Bible. The words *sheep* and *lamb* are mentioned more than four hundred times. Sheep are not smart and need a shepherd. The sheep learn to respond to their own shepherd's voice. If they get mixed up with another flock, the shepherds call them and they go to the right shepherd.

TRY IT

Let one person be a shepherd, and play Follow the Shepherd. Talk about following Jesus.

CHRISTMAS SYMBOL: SHEEP AND ANIMALS

He will stand and shepherd his flock in the strength of the Lord, in the majesty of the name of the Lord his God. They will dwell secure, because he will surely become great throughout the earth. Micah 5:4

The prophet Micah, who foretold that the birth of Jesus would take place in Bethlehem, also wrote that the Messiah would shepherd his people. Jesus is called the Good Shepherd. Jesus also is called the Lamb of God, because he is the pure sacrifice. He came to give himself for us.

Animals in the Nativity set and animal ornaments are popular decorations. Sheep are the only animals actually mentioned at the birth of Jesus, when we're told that shepherds were keeping watch over their flock. We fill Nativity sets with other animals, because the place with the manger suggests other animals slept there.

Sheep are not very bright and wander off easily. They need a shepherd. We can be like sheep and not make good choices. We need Jesus, our Good Shepherd.

TRY IT

Play the Sheep Roundup Game. Use cotton balls for sheep and a bowl for the pen. Blindfold a player to be the shepherd. Put the pen on the shepherd's lap. Have the shepherd use a spoon as a staff and try to scoop up sheep from a tabletop and put them in the pen.

Angelic News

The angel said, "Don't be afraid! Look! I bring good news to you—wonderful, joyous news for all people." Luke 2:10

SHEPHERDS HEARD news of great joy from the angels. How do you react to good news? Do you jump for joy or leap around like a happy lamb? Do you smile and shout or give someone a high-five? The shepherds talked and said, "Let's go right now to Bethlehem and see..." They wanted to see the wonder with their own eyes. Ignoring the news would be like leaving a gift wrapped up and never opening it!

They didn't dawdle. Different Bible translations use various words, but they all mean to go fast, hurry, go in haste, or run. Moving fast shows us the joy they felt. They found the baby lying in a manger and then returned home.

The shepherds didn't keep quiet. They spread the news. People who heard the shepherds wondered about what they heard, but the shepherds praised God. They knew the truth.

The angels said the news would bring great joy to all people. God wants us to spread the news that Jesus came. That will spread joy.

PRAYER

Lord, fill our hearts with joy. Help us be brave and happy to share the news and wish others a Merry Christmas. Amen.

HYMN/SONG

"Joy to the World"

QUESTIONS

- When have you shared good news?
- What makes you joyful?
- How can you share the news of the birth of Jesus?

DID YOU KNOW?

There is evidence that early Christians secretly met in the catacombs of Rome, Italy. These are tunnels that were used as burial places for people. Christian symbols, including drawings of sheep, are still visible on the walls.

TRY IT

Talk to someone about Jesus this week.

CHRISTMAS SYMBOL: CANDY CANE

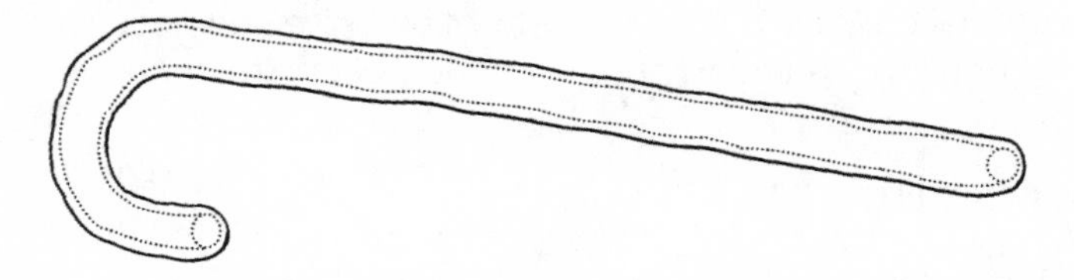

The LORD is my shepherd. I lack nothing. Psalm 23:1

There are many stories about the candy cane, and most of them are legends. There is no historical evidence of why they were made and bent into the well-known shape. Candy makers in Chicago, the Bunte Brothers, filed the first patent for candy cane making machines. These machines did not bend the canes. Originally, candy canes were white. The stripes were not blended in until the early part of the twentieth century.

People made bent candy canes by hand until 1950, when a priest in Georgia named Gregory Harding Keller invented a machine that twisted the colors, plus bent and cut the candy canes.

It's great to think of all the different meanings people now associate with the famous candy. It's wonderful to know we can use something simple to talk about Jesus. The shape looks like a shepherd's staff or the letter J, for Jesus. The colors of the canes have become reminders of Jesus—white for the purity of Jesus, and red because Jesus died for us.

TRY IT

Pass out candy canes and tell others what a candy cane makes you think about.

The Reason for the Season

Your savior is born today in David's city. He is Christ the Lord. Luke 2:11

THE ANGEL explained the reason to rejoice at the birth of Jesus. The angel stated it simply with the words *savior* and *Christ*. *Savior* means "one who delivers his people." *Christ* is the Greek word for "Anointed One." The Hebrew word is *Messiah*. *Lord* means "ruler."

Anointed means "to be set apart by God." It also means that God's Holy Spirit is upon the person. When Jesus spoke in the synagogue (Luke 4:14-30), he quoted Isaiah 61:1-2: "The LORD God's spirit is upon me, because the LORD has anointed me...." Jesus is God's chosen one.

The three names summed up the reason Jesus came. He is God who came to live among us. He came to give us eternal life.

"Your savior" reminds us that Jesus came for us, for each and every person. We are not perfect and need help, the help of Jesus. Memorize Luke 2:11, the reason for joy at Christmas.

PRAYER

Lord Jesus, Anointed One, Savior, we rejoice that you came. You are the reason we rejoice. Amen.

HYMN/SONG

"Good Christian Friends, Rejoice"

QUESTIONS

- What does the word *savior* mean to you?
- What helps you remember a Scripture? Try saying Luke 2:11 from memory.
- What gets you excited about the birth of Jesus? What helps you talk about it?

DID YOU KNOW?

In 1885, Wilson Alwyn Bentley perfected a process to catch snowflakes on black velvet and photograph them before they melted. His photos showed the uniqueness of each individual snowflake.

TRY IT

Make a paper snowflake.

1. Cut out a large paper circle.
2. Fold the circle in half three times.
3. Snip out little circles and triangles.
4. Open the paper to see your unique snowflake.

CHRISTMAS SYMBOL: SNOWFLAKES

Come now, and let's settle this, says the Lord. Though your sins are like scarlet, they will be white as snow. If they are red as crimson, they will become like wool. Isaiah 1:18

The angels appeared at night, but we don't really know the date of the birth of Jesus or the season. We celebrate it in winter in the United States, and for many that's a cold time when snow might fall. Many decorations include snowflakes, which ties into Isaiah 1:18 and Jesus being our Lord who forgives our sins.

A snowflake falls from the sky, unique and delicate. Jesus is the one who changes us and forgives our sins to make us pure and holy.

TRY IT

Make several paper snowflakes. Pinch the center of each one, and wrap one end of a chenille stem around it to form a flower with a stem. Place the flowers in a vase as a bouquet and reminder of what Jesus does for us.

A Sign for You

This is a sign for you: you will find a newborn baby wrapped snugly and lying in a manger. Luke 2:12

THE ANGEL gave the shepherds specific directions. They would find the infant wrapped in swaddling cloth and lying in a manger. The sign would be proof of the truth of the words. The shepherds listened and checked it out. They searched for the baby lying in a manger and found him.

The verse reminds us that everything God said is true. God invites us to examine God's promises. After Jesus rose, the early Christians searched the Scriptures daily to verify the truth (Acts 17:11).

The Greek word for *truth* is *aletheia*. It means to un-hide or hide nothing. Truth means the real facts about something. Truths about God do not change. We can rejoice that Jesus is the truth and that the shepherds confirmed the truth of his birth.

Faith means believing what we cannot see. We cannot go back and see Jesus as a baby, but we can believe the reports of the shepherds.

PRAYER

Lord, thank you for the Bible, which contains the truth. Help us examine it and follow it. Amen.

HYMN/SONG

"The First Noel"

QUESTIONS

- What happens when you don't tell the truth?
- What did the shepherds find in Bethlehem that helped them know that the angels spoke the truth?
- How do you study the Bible? What helps you see how it applies to your life?

DID YOU KNOW?

The *X* in *Xmas* uses a Greek letter *chi* for *Jesus*. People started writing Xmas in the 1500s as a symbol for Christ.

TRY IT

Photocopy, cut out, and decorate the *X* below. Then hang the X on your tree.

CHRISTMAS SYMBOL: CHRISMONS OR CHRIST MONOGRAMS

You, Bethlehem, land of Judah, by no means are you least among the rulers of Judah, because from you will come one who governs, who will shepherd my people Israel. Matthew 2:6

There are many symbols for Jesus, such as a shepherd's staff and a crown. These symbols reflect descriptions for Jesus in the Bible. The words in Matthew about Jesus as a ruler and shepherd came from Jewish scholars who helped the magi find the newborn King. They found the words in Micah 5:2.

In 1957, a woman named Frances Kipps Spencer decided to decorate a Christmas tree with white and gold symbols that represent Jesus. The white represents the purity of Jesus, and the gold represents his royalty as king. These decorations are known as Chrismons or Christ monograms. One of the oldest symbols for Jesus combines two Greek letters *chi* (*X*) and *rho* (*P*). Those are the first two letters of the word *Christos*, which means Christ.

Other Chrismons include a shepherd's staff, crown, star, cross, scroll, praying hands, heart, and fish. Look up more symbols and see how each one helps you think about Jesus.

TRY IT

Make a shepherd's staff Chrismon by twisting gold and white chenille stems together and bending them into a cane shape.

The Family of Jesus

A record of the ancestors of Jesus Christ, son of David, son of Abraham. Matthew 1:1

KING DAVID didn't spend his childhood in a palace. He grew up as a shepherd and spent many nights under the stars. God chose him to be king when he was a young shepherd. The prophet Samuel anointed David as the new king of Israel.

David fought the giant Goliath to save his people. He used his sling, the normal weapon of a shepherd. His courage to fight the giant Philistine came from God. The talents David developed, as he trusted God against other enemies, helped him trust God when he fought the giant. He said, "The LORD, who rescued me from the power of both lions and bears, will rescue me from the power of this Philistine." The sling worked well. David swung it around and shot a smooth pebble from it to slay Goliath.

David is in the family tree of Jesus, one of the people in Mary's line of names. Read the names in the first chapter of Matthew, and then look up and talk about some of them. Jesus has a big family tree.

PRAYER

Lord, thank you for all our families. Thanks for making us part of your family, too. Amen.

HYMN/SONG

"Christmas in Our Hearts"

QUESTIONS

- What names in the family tree of Jesus do you recognize? What did each one do?
- When did you do something brave? How can that help you be brave again?
- Talk about the birthplaces of each member of your family. What is important about each place?

DID YOU KNOW?

The family tree of Jesus names two women who were not Jewish. One is Rahab, who hid Israelite spies (Joshua 2). The other is Ruth, who married Boaz (Book of Ruth).

TRY IT

Use tiny tree branches to make a cross to hang on your Christmas tree. Make one or two photocopies of the crown on page 51, cut them out, decorate them, and attach them to the cross for King David and for Jesus (the newborn King).

CHRISTMAS SYMBOL: FAMILY TREE

But those who did welcome him, those who believed in his name, he authorized to become God's children. John 1:12

God wants an enormous, gigantic family. Anyone who believes in Jesus is welcomed into God's family. God adopts us. When we gather at church, we are coming together with part of God's family. That makes each believer at church part of God's big family and therefore your big family. When you have a meal at church, you're having a big family meal.

Christmas is a time to enjoy your own family traditions and special foods. Parents, siblings, grandparents, cousins, aunts, and uncles are all special members of your family. Look through photo albums at people from your family and chat about ones who lived before you were born. Notice if anyone was adopted. Learn something new about each family member. At church, greet people and learn about them.

Pray for your family, including your church family.

TRY IT

Put up a tree for photos, and add photos of family members and of ancestors.

The Real Red of Christmas

She approached at that very moment and began to praise God and to speak about Jesus to everyone who was looking forward to the redemption of Jerusalem. Luke 2:38

GOD CHOSE an eighty-four-year-old woman named Anna to meet the infant Jesus when Mary and Joseph brought him to the temple.

Anna's husband died years before the birth of Jesus. Anna spent many years in the temple, where she prayed and fasted daily. The Scriptures call Anna a prophet. Prophets spoke the truth about God. Sometimes prophets brought messages from God. Anna brought the message that this child would be the one to set God's people free.

God's plan to save us is sometimes called the scarlet thread of redemption. Rahab, a woman in Jericho, hung a red thread (or rope) from her window during the battle of Jericho. Joshua saved her when Jericho was destroyed. You'll find Rahab's name in the line of Jesus. The real red of Christmas is how Jesus loves us and saves us.

PRAYER

Lord Jesus, thank you for faithful people who serve you. Help us be faithful in prayer and in serving you. Amen.

HYMN/SONG

"O Come, Little Children"

QUESTIONS

- Why do you think God chose Anna?
- Why is it important that different people saw Jesus as a baby and recognized him as the Savior?
- Why is it important to remember at Christmas that Jesus came to save us?

DID YOU KNOW?

Look up Rahab and the red thread in Joshua 2. She is in the family line of Jesus.

TRY IT

Use a red marker and paper to list some of the promises about Jesus.

CHRISTMAS SYMBOL: RED BOWS

This is my blood of the covenant, which is poured out for many so that their sins may be forgiven. Matthew 26:28

Red is a color we use a lot at Christmas. This reflects the blood Jesus shed for us. Red also is used as a color for love. People trim trees with red ribbons and red bows. Some people place one red bow on their tree for each person in their family who has gone to heaven.

Red also is the color of some wines. At the Last Supper, Jesus held up a cup filled with wine. He blessed it and called it the blood of the covenant. *Covenant* is a special word for a promise. Jesus used it to show he was fulfilling God the Father's promise to send a savior to forgive our sins.

When you see a red bow, think of Jesus and what he did for you.

TRY IT

Make bows from red ribbons, or use a long red ribbon to decorate a tree, staircase, or wreath.

Celebrating the Birth

Simeon took Jesus in his arms and praised God. He said, "Now, master, let your servant go in peace according to your word, because my eyes have seen your salvation. You prepared this salvation in the presence of all peoples. It's a light for revelation to the Gentiles and a glory for your people Israel." Luke 2:28-32

AN OLD MAN named Simeon also saw Jesus as a baby and even held him. The Holy Spirit had promised that Simeon would live to see the Savior. He waited many years and continued to trust God. He expressed great joy as he proclaimed that the baby he held was the promised Savior.

Parents brought their babies to the temple at eight days old. Simeon probably saw many babies through the years, but he knew that Jesus was different. He declared Jesus to be the light for all and the glory of Israel.

Christmas celebrates how God keeps promises, that God sent a savior, and that Jesus is the light we all need. We may not know the actual date or time of day of the birth, but we can be happy it happened. Turn on the lights and rejoice!

PRAYER

Lord, thank you for coming. Help our hearts be happy at Christmas. Amen.

HYMN/SONG

"Silent Night"

QUESTIONS

- What facts can you name about the birth of Jesus?
- What helps you remember that Jesus is the reason for Christmas?
- What are some reasons Jesus came?

DID YOU KNOW?

Joseph and Mary brought Jesus to the temple in Jerusalem. King Herod had rebuilt the temple, which had many rooms. Only the high priest could enter the innermost part of the temple, and only once a year. Jewish men and women could enter the court of women. Men considered clean could go a little farther into the temple.

TRY IT

Wrap a little box in Christmas paper. Place verses in it that help you celebrate Christmas. Take one out to read aloud each day.

CHRISTMAS SYMBOL: CRÈCHE

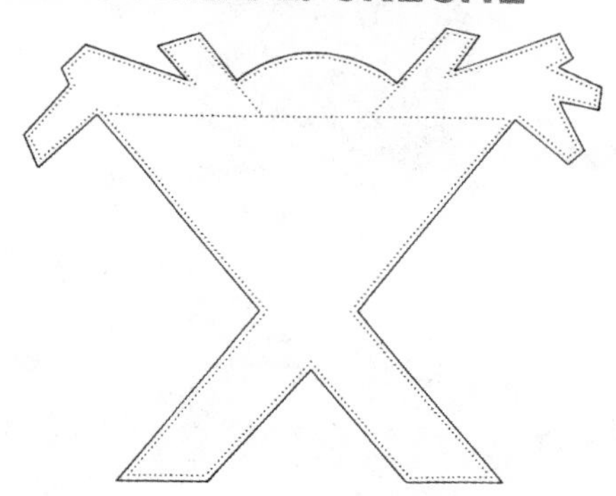

The Word became flesh and made his home among us. We have seen his glory, glory like that of a father's only son, full of grace and truth. John 1:14

An old word for *manger* is *crèche*, which is a French word. In Mexico, children wait until Christmas to lay the statue of Jesus in the crèche. During Advent they add pieces of straw for each good deed they do. They want lots of straw to give the baby a soft bed of hay.

The crèche makes a good display around which to celebrate the birth of Jesus. Many people hold a birthday party for Jesus. They may do this on Christmas morning or any time during Advent.

TRY IT

Plan a birthday party for Jesus. Consider using crowns or halos made from garlands as party hats, eating angel food cake, singing "Happy Birthday," and playing games related to a trip to Bethlehem, shepherds, and angels.

Peace
The Angel Candle

The Lord's angel stood before them, the Lord's glory shone around them, and they were terrified. Luke 2:9

THE LAST WEEK of Advent begins on a Sunday and goes until Christmas Day. It might last one to seven days. Light all four candles and notice the greater glow. The fourth candle is called the Candle of Peace and also the Angel Candle. The angels brought a message of peace.

The Lord's glory (a bright light) shone around the shepherds. Ezekiel 43:2 tells us that the Lord's glory even lights up the earth. The brightness and appearance of an angel terrified the shepherds. The angel's first words, "Don't be afraid," helped calm them.

When the sky filled with angels, they praised God and proclaimed peace among people in whom God is pleased. God is pleased when we believe in Jesus, follow God's rules, do good deeds, and share with others. Remember the words of the angels to not be afraid. You let the light of God's glory shine through your heart by loving others.

PRAYER

Lord, help us live in a way that pleases you. Amen.

HYMN/SONG

"Hark! the Herald Angels Sing"

QUESTIONS

- What do Colossians 1:10 and Hebrews 13:16 tell us pleases God?
- How can you live in peace this week?
- What is the brightest light you ever saw? The Lord's glory is brighter.

DID YOU KNOW?

The word *angel* means "messenger." God sent angels to deliver messages. Angels are mentioned at least 270 times in the Bible. Read Job 38:1-7 and you'll discover what angels did when they saw God create the earth. Revelation 14:6 refers to angels in flight.

TRY IT

Copy, cut out, and decorate the angel pattern. Add the paper angel to this week's candle.

CHRISTMAS SYMBOL: ANGEL

When Elizabeth was six months pregnant, God sent the angel Gabriel to Nazareth, a city in Galilee. Luke 1:26

We don't know what angels really look like. Sometimes they appear as people. We know they played an important part in the birth of Jesus. People place angel figurines as decorations on tables or with the Nativity set. Many people use an angel ornament as a tree topper. The custom began long ago to symbolize the angels appearing in the sky, above the shepherds in the fields.

Jesus mentioned that angels in heaven rejoice when one sinner repents. We know they praised God while shepherds looked at them. Angels are powerful (Psalm 103:20) and protect us (Matthew 18:10). Jesus said that, like the angels, believers will be raised from the dead and will not die in the future, after the resurrection of the dead (Luke 20:36). God wants us to follow the example of the angels and praise God and share the good news.

TRY IT

Make a paper angel from a doily (see page 87). Shine a light through the angel as a reminder of God's glory shining around them.

1

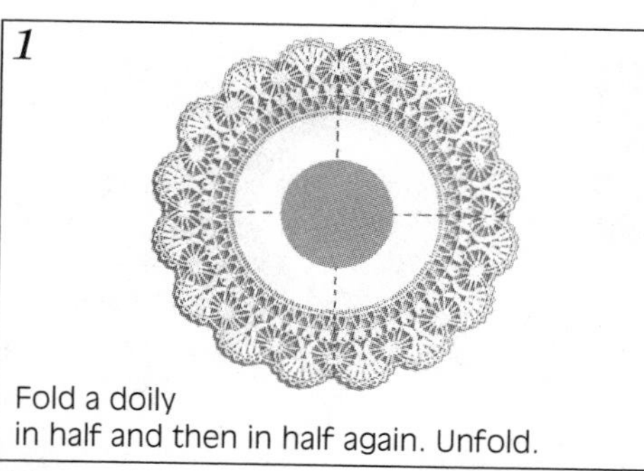

Fold a doily
in half and then in half again. Unfold.

2

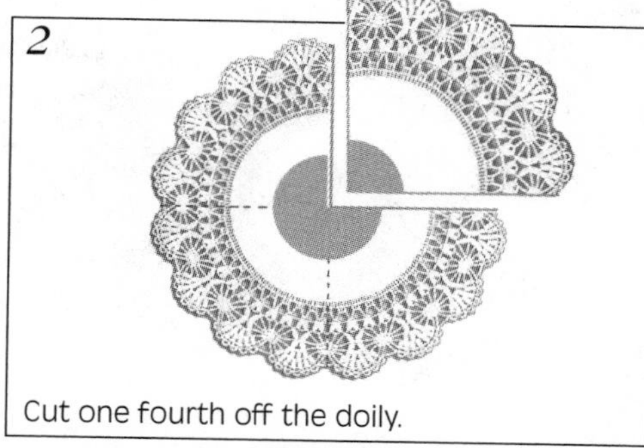

Cut one fourth off the doily.

3

Cut that one-fourth piece in half.

4

Fold the three-fourths doily on the fold lines, then glue it in place.

5

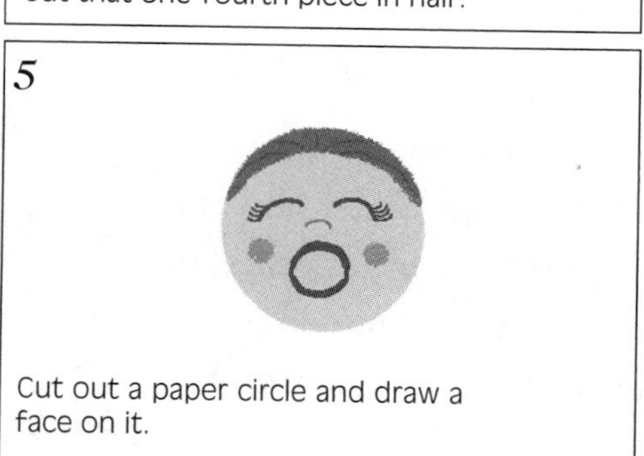

Cut out a paper circle and draw a face on it.

6

Glue the face on top of the folded doily.

7

Glue the two small pieces (wings) to the back of the doily angel.

Peace on Earth

A child is born to us, a son is given to us, and authority will be on his shoulders. He will be named Wonderful Counselor, Mighty God, Eternal Father, Prince of Peace. Isaiah 9:6

ON THE FIRST CHRISTMAS, angels proclaimed peace on earth. Long before the birth of Jesus, Isaiah called him the Prince of Peace and other names. Jesus can bring peace to our hearts, even when there are problems and trouble in the world. You need to light the candle for it to glow. So, too, you must do your part to bring peace to the world.

Begin spreading peace in your home by serving and loving one another. Ask God to give you inner peace, and choose to forgive anyone who hurt you. If you feel angry, pause to take a deep breath to become calmer, and then try to settle things peacefully. Choose to be thankful each day, thanking God for all you have and expressing gratitude to anyone who is kind to you. Remember that a happy heart lessens whining and helps you feel like smiling.

PRAYER

Lord, give us peace in our hearts and help us each work to be peacemakers. Amen.

HYMN/SONG

"Let There Be Peace on Earth"

QUESTIONS

- What can you do to have peace in your home?
- How can you decorate with doves, a symbol of peace?
- How does forgiving others help you have a happy heart?

DID YOU KNOW?

The dove is one of the earliest symbols in the Bible, going back to Noah and the ark (Genesis 8:10-12). It was a popular early symbol of Christians that was used four centuries before the cross became a common symbol of faith in Christ. Dove implements included dove oil lamps and holders for Communion. Other religions and temples to idols also used doves.

TRY IT

Print some cards that say "Peace on earth" or "Thanks for your kindness." Pass them out to people who are kind or who might need peace.

CHRISTMAS SYMBOL: DOVE

John [the Baptist] testified, "I saw the Spirit coming down from heaven like a dove, and it rested on him [Jesus]. John 1:32

The cooing of a dove is a soft lulling sound that people often find soothing or comforting. A dove is considered a symbol of the Holy Spirit and of peace. It's one of the first birds named in the Bible. After the flood, Noah sent a raven out of the ark to see if the ground had dried. Next, Noah sent a dove to check the earth. The bird returned with a freshly picked olive leaf. The dove helped Noah know that the earth had dried up. Soon afterward, God told Noah to come out of the ark and made a promise to Noah never to flood the entire earth again. The dove has been used in other ways to symbolize peace.

God asked his people to offer sacrifices that included a dove. The dove served as a substitute sacrifice for poor people, who could not afford to give a lamb. Mary and Joseph brought doves to the temple as an offering when they first brought Jesus there.

At the baptism of Jesus, the heavens opened and the Holy Spirit descended in the form of a dove.

TRY IT

Copy, cut out, and fold page 91 to make paper doves that can fly (like paper airplanes). Write on them words of promises to be peacemakers. Nestle them in your Christmas wreath or tree.

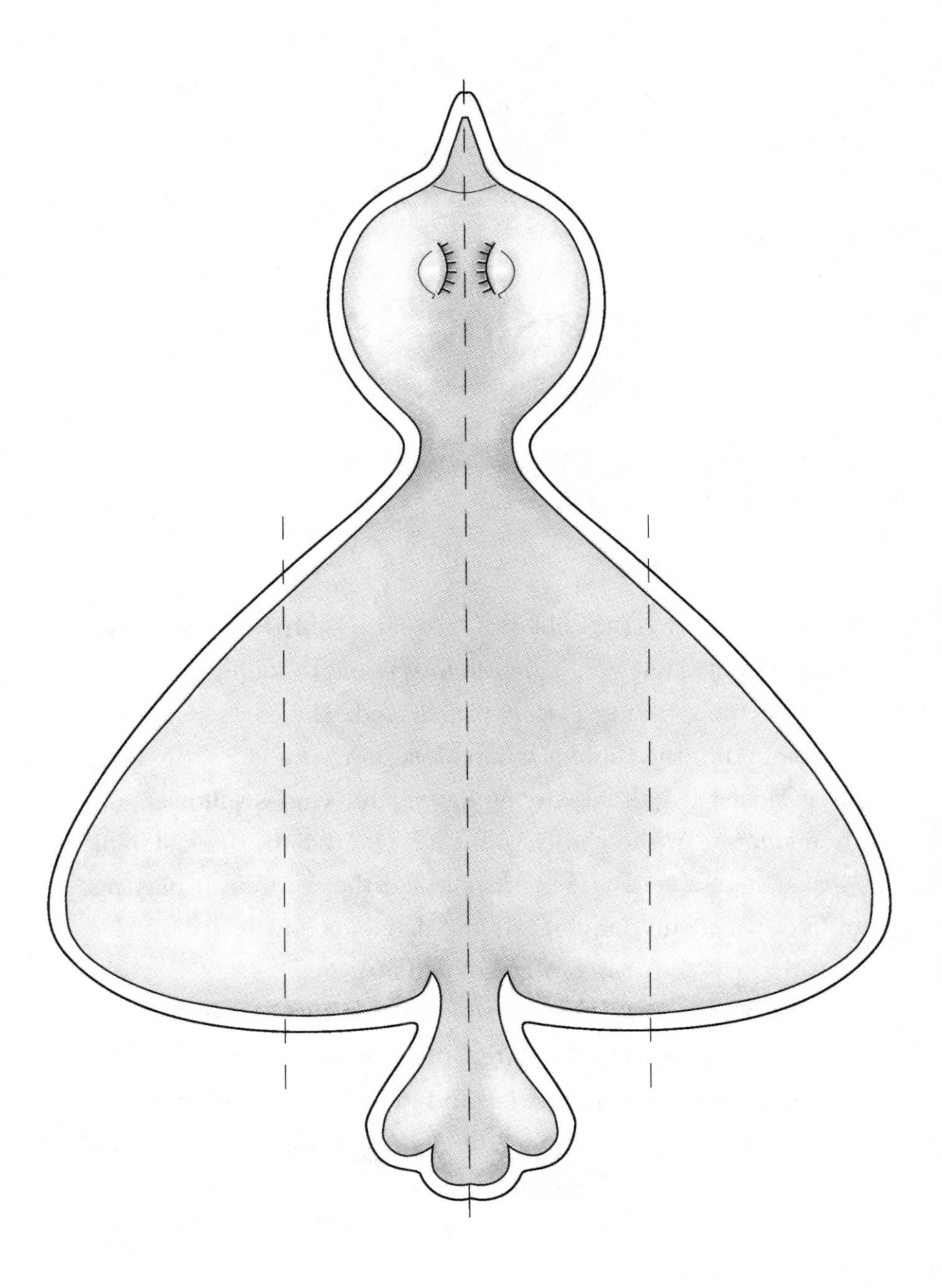

Praising God

Glory to God in heaven, and on earth peace among those whom he favors. Luke 2:14

VOICES OF ANGELS filled the sky at the birth of Jesus and praised God. That's an example for people to follow.

Many people sing as they praise God. The earliest singing mentioned in the Bible is when Moses and the Israelites sang after Moses led them out of Egypt and God swallowed up their enemy in the sea (Exodus 15:1). Miriam, the sister of Moses, sang a second song as she led the women in playing tambourines and dancing. As the disciples and Jesus left the Last Supper, they sang (Matthew 26:30).

The word *carol* comes from the Latin word *choraula*, meaning "to dance to the flute," or from the old French word *caroler*, meaning "dancing around in a circle." Singing songs for neighbors dates back to the eighth or ninth century. In 1223, St. Francis of Assisi included songs or "canticles" in the Nativity plays. In time, people started traveling from house to house to sing carols. Play or sing Christmas songs to rejoice, praise God, and share the message of Christmas.

PRAYER

Lord, thanks for giving us music and voices that can sing. Help us use songs to praise you. Amen.

HYMN/SONG

"Lo, How a Rose E'er Blooming"

QUESTIONS

- What Christmas carols do you like? Make a list of your favorite carols and look up facts about each one.
- Talk about the words of a favorite Christmas carol.
- When do you like to sing or to listen to music?

DID YOU KNOW?

One of the earliest lists of carols, in 1426 by John Awdlay, lists twenty-five songs. "The Holly and the Ivy" is one of the oldest musical compositions still sung regularly. Museum collectors in the nineteenth century started discovering early carols in museums. They found more than 500.

TRY IT

Make up your own carol or write new words to a familiar tune.

CHRISTMAS SYMBOL: CAROLERS

Be glad in the Lord always! Again I say, be glad!
Philippians 4:4

To go with the caroling, people started making carved figures of carolers to add to their decorations. These figures often are dressed in clothing of the Victorian period of England, when caroling became very popular.

In England, Puritan laws banned caroling in 1647, but people continued to sing in secret. In 1660, the law was declared null and void, and carolers once again filled streets with music praising God. Laws cannot keep people from having joy in their hearts or singing in their minds.

Opening a door to hear carolers sing can be a joyous experience. It also lifts our spirits when we sing or listen to praise music. When we reflect on the words of the carols, we can rejoice in all the wonder of what happened that first Christmas.

The joy of carols can be seen in figurines of carolers and children in choir robes. Carolers sing out praise to God and share the news of the birth of Jesus through the words in the songs. They show joy with their smiles and happy voices.

TRY IT

Gather with friends and go caroling, or hold an indoor caroling party.

Trumpets, Bells, and Music

With trumpets and a horn blast, shout triumphantly before the LORD, the king! Psalm 98:6

PSALM 98 often is read on Christmas Day, as it affirms the reign of God. For early Christians, Jesus was the King and Messiah, who brought God's reign to all people. These first Christians sang Psalm 98 as a song about Jesus. Music is part of praising God, and several Psalms include making joyful noises and playing instruments.

In ancient times, people used animal horns to blow a blast. Shofar is the name for the instruments made from horns and used for religious ceremonies. The noise of a shofar from the cloud on Mount Sinai during the time of Moses caused people to tremble (Exodus 19:16). Israelite armies used the shofar as an alarm in battle. It is blown in synagogues for Rosh Hashanah and Yom Kippur.

PRAYER

Lord Jesus, we praise you with the sound of trumpets and music. Amen.

HYMN/SONG

"Who Would Imagine a King?" or "From Heaven Above to Earth I Come"

QUESTIONS

- What instruments do you enjoy hearing and why?
- How does music add to a celebration? What are favorite songs you sing at church?
- What do you think about Christ returning? Are you ready?

DID YOU KNOW?

King David wrote many of the Psalms. They are considered to be songs. David played the harp. Bible instruments include tambourines, flutes, trumpets, cymbals, castanets, pipes, timbrels, bagpipes, lyres, and horns.

TRY IT

Make a joyful noise with instruments, party horns, or kitchen objects.

CHRISTMAS SYMBOL TRUMPETS AND MUSICAL INSTRUMENTS

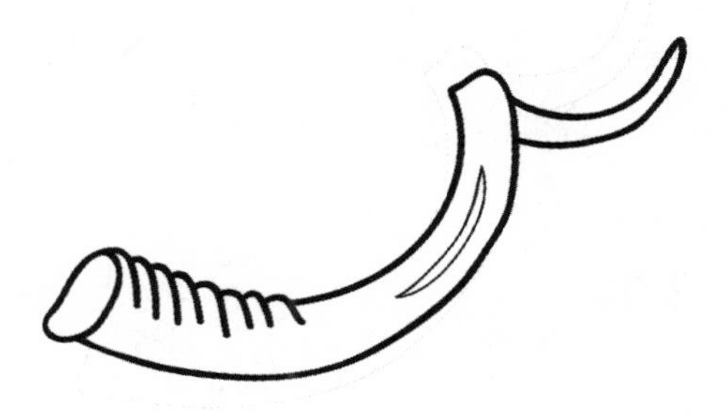

He will send his angels with the sound of a great trumpet, and they will gather his chosen ones from the four corners of the earth, from one end of the sky to the other. Matthew 24:31

God established a special day in the fall called the Feast of Trumpets, which is known as Rosh Hashanah. It's a time of rest and atonement.

But angels blowing trumpets are not mentioned in the Bible at the birth of Christ. The angels filled the sky with their voices. It must have been a beautiful sound. The shepherds praised God that day, adding more joyful noise to glorify God. Psalm 150 reminds us to praise God. It mentions many musical instruments and also states, "Let every living thing praise the LORD!"

TRY IT

Copy, cut out, and decorate the paper instruments on page 98 to hang on the Christmas tree.

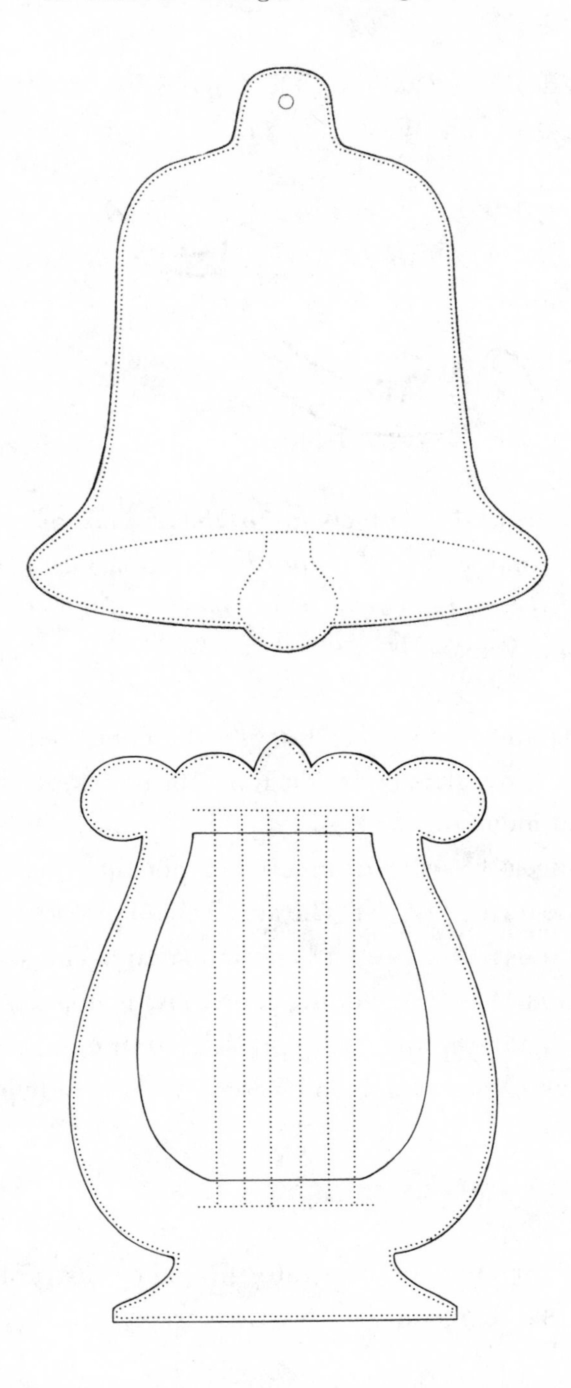

Filled With God's Spirit

When Elizabeth heard Mary's greeting, the child leaped in her womb, and Elizabeth was filled with the Holy Spirit. Luke 1:41

WHAT DO you do when you're happy? Do you jump for joy, give a high-five, shout "Hooray!" or dance around? Do you know that you may have jumped at a very young age?

God filled Elizabeth with the Holy Spirit when she greeted Mary. Your mom can probably tell you about times you kicked her as you grew in her womb or maybe jumped inside her. If you're adopted, your mom can recall the first time you showed excitement or jumped with joy.

Elizabeth cried out to Mary, "God has blessed you above all women, and he has blessed the child you carry." Elizabeth knew that God chose Mary to be the mother of God's Son.

In the Old Testament, God's Spirit came to a few people; but once Pentecost came, God sent the Holy Spirit to all believers. Jesus called the Holy Spirit the Companion (or Helper). Jesus told us that the Helper will be our teacher and will help us remember God.

PRAYER

Lord, thanks for sending us a Helper, the Holy Spirit. Amen.

HYMN/SONG

"What Child Is This?"

QUESTIONS

- Talk about the Holy Spirit. Why did Jesus send the Helper (Companion)? (Look up John 14.)
- What happens as a child grows inside his or her mother?
- What did Elizabeth's baby do when Mary visited?

DID YOU KNOW?

Moms don't usually feel a baby move inside the womb until the baby has been growing for four to five months.

TRY IT

Look at your baby photos and listen to your parents' stories about you.

CHRISTMAS SYMBOL: CHRISTMAS STOCKING

Why do I have this honor, that the mother of my Lord should come to me? As soon as I heard your greeting, the baby in my womb jumped for joy. Luke 1:43-44

Many legends exist about stockings being filled with treats or gold. Colorful and fancy stockings are a familiar sight these days. Long ago, most people had only a few items of clothing. They would wash and hang them to dry near the fire, on a mantel if they had one. A mother could slip a treat inside the sock as it dried.

In some countries such as Holland and Italy, children left their shoes out in hopes of having a treat placed inside it on Christmas Eve. These customs also bring in Santa Claus or Kris Kringle that came from legends of a saintly man who wanted to help out some poor young maidens.

It can be good to change a tradition to use it as a symbol for faith. Christmas stockings can be filled, and so can our hearts. It's easy to compare being filled with God's love and the Holy Spirit to filling a stocking.

TRY IT

As you pull out contents of stockings this year, talk about being filled with God's love and God's Holy Spirit. Make joyful noises as you find a special treat or treasure. Praise God with words that express your love for God and your awe of God's greatness.

Heavenly Sign

They asked, "Where is the newborn king of the Jews? We've seen his star in the east, and we've come to honor him." Matthew 2:2

MAGI FROM THE EAST traveled to Jerusalem because they saw an unusual star in the sky. These men were not Jews, but gentiles who searched for truth. They followed the heavenly star until it disappeared from their view.

These magi believed this special star would lead them to a newborn King. They stopped at the palace of King Herod. The king called his scholars. Jewish priests and scribes pointed out the words of prophecy, naming Bethlehem as the prophesied location of the promised King. The magi started toward Bethlehem, and the star appeared again. They found Jesus, the King. He was not in a stable, but in a house, for the men had traveled and searched a long time. They did not worship the star, but they did worship Jesus.

We must look up to see stars. So, too, we must look for the Christ, the true light. We can find Christ in the Bible, in our hearts, and through our prayers.

PRAYER

Lord, help us see truth and follow you. Truth is found in your Word. Amen.

HYMN/SONG

"We Three Kings"

QUESTIONS

- What truth have you found in the Bible?
- How do stars and constellations help guide sailors and other travelers?
- These magi (wise men) who found Jesus are called wise. How are you wise?

DID YOU KNOW?

The star appeared at an exact time in history, it rose in the east (not all stars do that), it remained for a period of time, and it stopped at a specific place.

TRY IT

Make different-sized star sugar cookies. Layer them with frosting to make a star Christmas tree. Or use a star cookie cutter to make star-shaped sandwiches.

CHRISTMAS SYMBOL: STAR

When they heard the king, they went; and look, the star they had seen in the east went ahead of them until it stood over the place where the child was. When they saw the star, they were filled with joy. Matthew 2:9-10.

Once the star stopped, the magi found Jesus and their hearts filled with joy. We don't need to see a star or Jesus to rejoice. First Peter 1:7-8 talks about the joy of believers who do not see Jesus, but believe and rejoice. Christmas is a time to rejoice and be amazed as we think about what happened in Bethlehem.

The twinkling light in the sky led to joyful hearts. It takes four light years for the light of the second nearest star to reach the earth. The nearest star is the sun. Unlike regular stars or planets in the sky, this star had the ability to stop and stay in one place. It was unlike anything else in the heavens. God set the right star in the sky at the exact moment so that the light would shine at the time of the birth of Jesus. Amazing!

We use a star at Christmas as a reminder of the magi, who came later to celebrate the birth of Jesus and to confirm his birth.

TRY IT

Copy, cut out, and decorate the star on page 105. Put the star over your door as a sign that your home is a place where Christ dwells. Use battery-operated lights to light up the star.

Gift Wrapped

She gave birth to her firstborn child, a son, wrapped him snugly, and laid him in a manger, because there was no place for them in the guestroom. Luke 2:7

THE ANGEL GAVE the shepherds a sign for finding the right baby. The announcement stated that they would find the baby wrapped in cloths and lying in a manger. This would confirm the words of the angel about the birth of the Savior.

Mary had wrapped Jesus in strips of cloth. The word used in Greek is *sparganoo*, which means "to clothe in strips of cloth." It was a custom to wrap a baby tightly and reflects the care Mary took of her new baby. In ancient times, the custom was done to help the baby's limbs grow straight. The wrapping is mentioned twice.

In contrast, one would expect a king to be dressed in royal robes. Yet the new King was found in swaddling clothes and in the unusually humble place of a manger. Lowly shepherds, unlikely choices as the first visitors to see Jesus and be witnesses to something so great, discovered a precious infant, more worthy than any other child ever born.

PRAYER

Lord, we are thankful for all the ways you confirmed the birth of Jesus. Amen.

HYMN/SONG

"It Came Upon the Midnight Clear"

QUESTIONS

- What have you noticed when you looked at a baby?
- What did the angel tell the shepherds?
- How do you know God cares about ordinary people and poor people?

DID YOU KNOW?

According to Micah 4:8, the angels appeared at a place known as the Tower of the Flock. The unblemished lambs born there were used for the sacrifices at the temple.

TRY IT

Play a game of hide the manger or the baby. Let the finder yell, "Praise God for sending Jesus!"

CHRISTMAS SYMBOL: GIFT WRAP

They entered the house and saw the child with Mary his mother. Falling to their knees, they honored him. Then they opened their treasure chests and presented him with gifts of gold, frankincense, and myrrh. Matthew 2:11

The magi brought precious gifts to honor Jesus. Jesus is a special gift for us. Each day as we read the Bible, we again receive the gift of Jesus in our life. Each blessing we receive comes from our Lord. Because we are blessed with such a great gift, we should reach out to share. Giving gifts at Christmas is one way to bless others.

As we give gifts to others, we take care to wrap them. Let wrapping gifts be a reminder of the care given to Jesus. Pray for the person receiving the gift so that the person is wrapped in prayer. The humble wrapping paper never compares to the gift of Jesus, but it opens doors for us to share the reason why we give gifts at Christmas.

We should make sure when we give a gift to someone that we express our love.

TRY IT

Make wrapping paper and gift tags.

- Use stamps, such as stars, angels, and mangers, on plain paper.
- Cut out shapes of Christmas symbols, and use them for gift tags.

Christmas Day
The Christ Candle

He will be great and he will be called the Son of the Most High. The Lord God will give him the throne of David his father. Luke 1:32

GOD'S LOVE came to earth in the form of Jesus at Christmas. On Christmas Day, we light one final candle. It's the Christ Candle, a white one that is placed in the center of the wreath. God should be at the center of Christmas. Jesus is the greatest gift and treasure ever! Treasure Christ's love now. Treasure Christ's love every day.

When the shepherds came and saw Jesus, Mary treasured the events of that night in her heart. She heard the shepherds glorify and praise God. She saw the promised child and held him. She didn't fully understand.

We don't always understand the ways of God or God's answers, but we can treasure God's words and wonders in our hearts. Each day as you read God's Word, ponder and treasure it.

PRAYER

God, thank you for sending such a wonderful gift. Amen.

HYMN/SONG

"Happy Birthday, Jesus"

QUESTIONS

- Why did God send Jesus?
- What helps you remember Jesus every day?
- What is the greatest treasure?

DID YOU KNOW?

We don't know the actual date of the birth of Jesus. Any day could be the real Christmas Day.

TRY IT

Begin a journal to keep notes of blessings, prayer answers, and Scriptures. Start by photocopying the Scriptures on page 112. Let your journal be a treasured keepsake.

CHRISTMAS SYMBOL: BABY JESUS

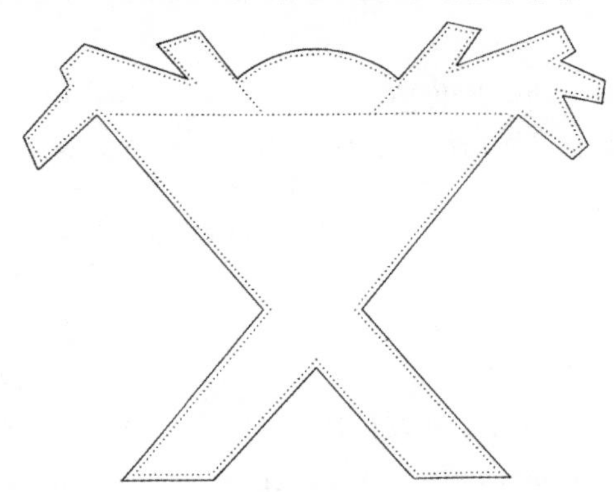

In the same way, let your light shine before people, so they can see the good things you do and praise your Father who is in heaven. Matthew 5:16

Many people wait until Christmas Day to place a figure of Jesus in the manger. It's the final touch that shows Christmas arrived and God fulfilled the promise to send a savior. We celebrated the good news and what we learned as we lit the candles on the Advent wreath.

We hope the glow from the candles will remind us of the glow of God's love in our hearts. Let that glow within show in your smile and life. Let the light from the Advent wreath and Christ Candle remind you to be lights and to spread the joy.

TRY IT

- Plan to place Jesus in the manger on Christmas morning. Sing "Happy Birthday" to Jesus.
- While decorations are up, take photos and add them to your journal or an album to look at and remember the treasures of the Christmas season.

Therefore, the Lord will give you a sign. The young woman is pregnant and is about to give birth to a son, and she will name him Immanuel. Isaiah 7:14

A child is born to us, a son is given to us, and authority will be on his shoulders. He will be named Wonderful Counselor, Mighty God, Eternal Father, Prince of Peace. Isaiah 9:6

She gave birth to her firstborn child, a son, wrapped him snugly, and laid him in a manger, because there was no place for them in the guestroom. Luke 2:7

The angel said, "Don't be afraid! Look! I bring good news to you—wonderful, joyous news for all people." Luke 2:10